THE WORLD'S MOST TERRIFYING PREDATORS

PART 1

By Justin & Peter Hoke

The World's Most Terrifying Predators Part 1

By Justin Hoke

To Sam, Peter, and Joshua

Printed in the United States of America

First Printing, 2023

The Lion

The lion lives in Africa and is known as the king of the jungle.

They eat meat, such as zebras and antelopes.

Lions are very strong and hunt in
groups called prides.

They can live up to 15 years.

The Tiger

The tiger lives in Asia and is the biggest cat in the world.

They eat meat, such as deer and wild pigs.

Tigers are very fast and sneaky when they hunt.

They can live up to 20 years.

The Crocodile

The crocodile lives in Africa, Asia, Australia, and America.

They eat meat, such as fish and other animals that come to drink at the river.

Crocodiles are very good swimmers and have very powerful jaws.

They can live up to 70 years.

The
Anaconda

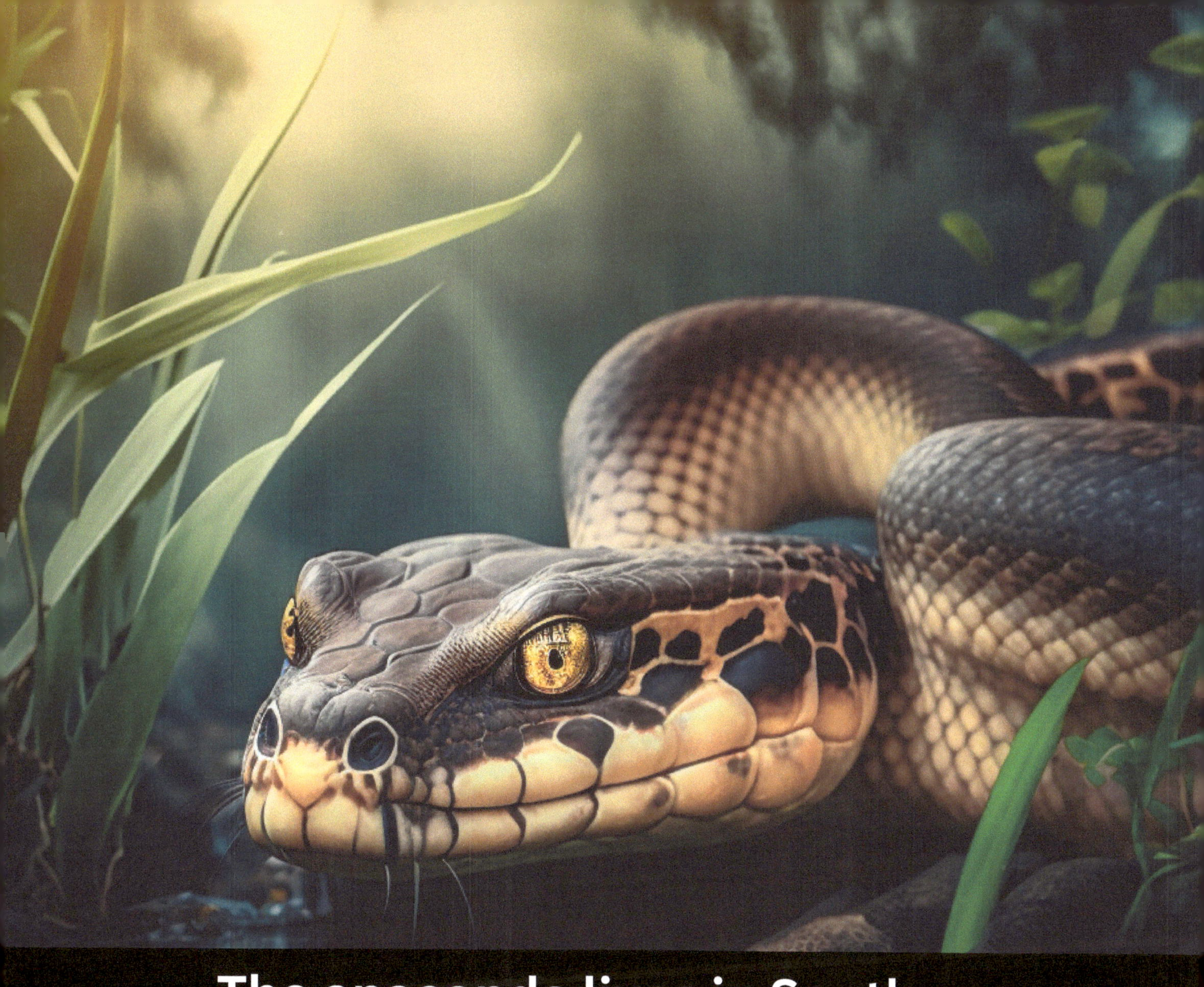

The anaconda lives in South America and is the biggest snake in the world.

They eat animals such as deer and caimans.

Anacondas are very good at squeezing their prey to death.

They can live up to 30 years.

The Grizzly Bear

The grizzly bear lives in North America.

They eat meat, such as salmon and other animals.

They are very strong and can run very fast.

They can live up to 25 years.

The Great white Shark

The great white shark lives in the ocean

They eat meat, such as seals and fish.

They are very good swimmers and can smell blood from very far away.

They can live up to 70 years.

The Polar Bear

The polar bear lives in the Arctic

They eat meat, such as seals and fish.

They are very good swimmers and their fur keeps them warm in the cold weather.

They can live up to 25 years.

THE END